PERENNIAL

PERENNIAL

Kelly Forsythe

COFFEE HOUSE PRESS

Minneapolis

2018

Coffee House Press books are available to the trade through our primary distributor, Consortium Book Sales & Distribution, cbsd.com or (800) 283-3572. For personal orders, catalogs, or other information, write to info@coffeehousepress.org.

Coffee House Press is a nonprofit literary publishing house. Support from private foundations, corporate giving programs, government programs, and generous individuals helps make the publication of our books possible. We gratefully acknowledge their support in detail in the back of this book.

LIBRARY OF CONGRESS CATALOGING-IN-PUBLICATION DATA

Names: Forsythe, Kelly, author.
Title: Perennial / Kelly Forsythe.
Description: Minneapolis : Coffee House Press, 2018. | Includes
    bibliographical references.
Identifiers: LCCN 2018000107 | ISBN 9781566895170 (trade pbk.)
Classification: LCC PS3606.O748664 A6 2018 | DDC 811/.6—dc23
LC record available at https://lccn.loc.gov/2018000107

PRINTED IN THE UNITED STATES OF AMERICA

25 24 23 22 21 20 19 18   1 2 3 4 5 6 7 8

Contents

PERENNIAL

Opening Doors

It started with two births
as quiet as pinpricks

two translucent ripples
in the Colorado River

or two white breezes
kicking up clay

& after the hospital,
they went home

& lived in their
mountains which

were supposed
to be merciful

but the air up there
tore its own breath away

& across the country, with
little to no surrender,
I removed myself from hiding

& my parents left a hospital
in Pittsburgh

where many others
were also born in April

& headed to their
home in the river

warm silences
resting between them

the good sun
hooking our eyelashes

& none of us had met yet

Historical Documents

I am writing an autobiography of myself as
a man. I want to use the word *excavate* here

I'll use *imagining* instead
as in   you see me imagining
deep unconscious feelings of manliness. Doesn't
everyone love tan shoulders? Doesn't

the wind feel good when you rush
into it—even in the Midwest when
the stars drop out of hiding into the black

it is catching it is
freezing & I'm sunburned

Meditation hasn't worked. We are writing
about the things we're afraid of. Your arms
your arms   you're giving everything away

Moral Panic

All boys have dreams.
Unhook. You took a short
drive & went to the hilltop.
To the cafeteria, the library,
bathrooms, the library. The fire
didn't light. Amber dried
on your upper lip, nose. Murder
an act of daylight
declaring itself against sun.

It is the way of things: the pollen—
it's hard not to take it
to heart, how it lands
against the

glass. You dream under
a poster of Jenny McCarthy, teen
dream. There were hundreds

of abandoned backpacks,
more than ninety bombs, match
strikers taped to your forearm.

They could smell gasoline
from the sidewalk of your home:
your parents know the absolute

price. Fingertips cut from a leather
glove in a wastebasket. It's
as if you struck

& from the moment
the match warned us
of your burning, we couldn't
contend. We had to bide.

Colony Collapse

There is a performance
in Kosovo. It strikes.
It strikes from March to June.
Someone puts their hand
on a window & yells: *how
many kings in this kingdom?*

That same year, we are made
to fear a game in which
dragons & dungeons
lead to unchecked occult
madness, Dr. Kevorkian
looming over a syringe.

It is the idea of calling
something blind though
you see how it carries
dust in window light.
It could be about safety.
I've asked more than once
what the longest bone in
our body is: it is *femur,* or
is it *fever,* or a panic of morals
& how we choose to run
to or from them. The tether
of our cells to her cells or his:

we can't help the connections.
We make them by falling. The
woman in the movie says how
much dress code matters. He
could be hiding a gun in his

baggy shorts. So then,
hiding. Or falling,

or the idea that by doing
both we have escaped
an inevitability. That
the very act of confronting,
of the face-off, leads to
something much darker—
a painted nail breaking
at the cuticle. Pink flower,
say goodbye: *goodbye!* Right
from the stem & gone.

1999

I clip my bangs back with a plastic butterfly. Under pajamas, I
wear a sports bra, white with tearing elastic, take it off only to
shower.

I hate my body this way it has become, need compression to bind
the newness flat into me. I'll say the same set of prayers tonight
and forgive myself for the AOL chat rooms. Lord, forgive me the
chat rooms. I am only an observer, I am only a witness to events.
I am only just now learning about Bill Clinton, and from this, the
idea of contempt, that one can be "held" in it, a cradle of derision
in the arms of a courtroom. Contempt in a classroom, also a kind
of holding.

The recoil from his shotgun caught him straight in the face,
breaking his nose, causing it to bleed. His face disturbed several
students, who told reporters afterward that he looked as though
he had been drinking blood.

Consider intentionally falsifying statements. In bed, I run my
tongue across my braces, rubber-banded black & gold, fall asleep
on my stomach in an effort to suppress.

Curved

There is no commitment
in the spring. Minerals
crush against other elements:
snow traces spills of water into
stars around grass, dirt
unwraps and rewraps by the roots
of cool oaks. I try to script

flowers, small as cursive, into
the creasing soil, but it is still
too cold, stripping. The stare
of the bulbs embarrasses me, the
responsibility, my palms unable
to warm their callow shells. I should
have been warned

about the flush of April, the false
green hanging limp on trees like broken
necklaces. I thought
these stems could settle
into the ground, try to untangle the chill
from bare, resisting earth,

smooth heat to swell the elm. Why
do we relieve the winter with so
much fatigue? The dragging rays
of the sun throw fractured light
onto the lawn, openly exhausted.
I thought I could shake the depletion,
intrude to wake the feathering melt.

Requiem

We were thinking of wetting the bed,
needle phobias, nervous tics, or how tenth
grade now means smoke in the AV room—

or in the West
a young man stands in a classroom
holding a bright but exhausted
malice: all the kids are cosmic surprises

with juice boxes & flower drawings

little are the pencils & erasers
little did we know
what it meant to really *burst forth*

or how many or how much
or how to stop
the trees from falling,
the smallest of our trees,

—which is
to say Columbine, which is
to say many things

Colorado, Hunting

I was in the midst
and the hill had the legs
and ears of sheep all over
its shaking grass. Tried

to run but the grief was
a cinder we stirred up
from trees. We

were in the midst
all the time. White
crimped wool
we found beside a log
full of density, soaked.
Everything on the ground
is breaking into milk teeth,
our bodies our bodies our
bodies. It changed the way
I look.

A poem in which I am dreaming

I have stickers on my arms by Lisa Frank.
Glitter on my shoulder. I turn and reflect
against a trophy case. Something else—you—
also in reflection. Two boys, boy, boy.

You both have hair like warm carpet,
I could hide under your hair.
I am shining with fake bear holograms.

I open the exit door and throw myself out
a window. The window was broken or
I broke it with my cheek. I land at two

pairs of shoes & look up to your
eyes but they are headphones.
My arms and legs are stuck together,

nothing moves except my hair. It
is blonde with glue. Both of you
lie down beside me. We watch clouds
to find bear shapes. I can feel us

wanting to hold hands. I roll onto
my side and fall off a chair, under
neath a table. On top a biology
textbook next to a yellow name tag.

Many yellow body tags, tags
on the floor next to caution tape.
I am still glued to myself. You
both are gone down some stairs
with the carpet torn out.

No, Everything

Down the hall, through
doors, exploring rooms

cloud-made chairs
sabotage the way
we rest.

We think a lot. How

our friends
are collapsing
under each other. We have

questions about bridges
which lie down constantly

good and bad movies,
how everything
connects but in a
separate curiosity,
everyone trying
to get higher and stable.

Today is a cycle: the
physical boundaries
of our bodies are cruel
against the shell of school—

if this is a cliff theory, we
are clinging onto
the smallest rocks.

Call to Action

Call us rebels. Call us
dark confiscations. Call us to
dinner. We're making movies,
we're making a plan, we're
following each other

around basements.
Watch the ascension of
anxiety, watch the appearance
of police, watch us

needing each other, watch
CNN. Will you pay attention
to our trench coats? Will you see

our shifting moods? Will you
mow the dry lawn? Will you
set up a dynamic

that is also an obsession?
Will you discuss patterns?
Will we believe in each

other's tendencies? Will
we see delusions for the sake

of our destiny? Do you want
to make a movie? Do you
want Spielberg to direct it?
Do we trust each other

for the sake of success?
Do you want to come
over? Call us civilians.

Call us red and now
call us speechless. Us:
dragging. Us: holding.
Us: turning. Us: marrow.
Us: bone. Us: ghost. Us:
breaking. Us: quiet. Us:
close. Us: holding.

Planner Notes, 7th grade

I charted proximity
between shivers.
It took a long time
to warm up, even sitting
next to a boy whose
skin looked like actual
silence. Actual gardens
of silent tulips. Poised
in its geometry.
Lord help me, English

class is only fifty minutes
long. We did not become
what I wanted but I was content
getting sick off ember vapors
illuminating your body. It was
to the point of hunger,
honestly, the demands

of my hormones—
frantic, a werewolf
in a palace of full moons.
I fumbled my way through
lessons on *Gatsby,* just staring
at his sleeves. It was enough
to diagram sentences
to consider the possibilities,
breaking up roots.
All of the mornings

in March I relearned
fluorescence by staring
straight into it, avoiding
eye contact. By the end
of April, we were
examining our own
potential for violence.
It wasn't that he was less
immaculate. Safety

had changed & no one
was ready; we were
hitting the windows
with our palms, asking
to be looked after
looked in on
we couldn't touch
each other for fear
of each other's unknowns.

We Are in a Room with Small Windows

after Graham Foust

In our hands and nails, shredded glass
and wire. The walls:
pared down and broken.

Up in the sunset, there are scraps—
a chip of bone, a contact, a pierced
earring.

Here we are, awake or
hurt. Here we are
or hurt.

To what face do we owe
this sameness? Not our cheeks
dusty and warm. Not that
any hand isn't already clenching.

The Skeptic

You sketched your outfit
with intimacy: block arrows
point to pockets of one-dimension,
empty & crossed by notebook lines.
Suspenders, cargo pants, punk gloves, a T-shirt
with "wrath" on the front. Snapple
bottle with gas & oil in a camera pouch.

Drew these clothes on a body
where your face is a white circle
of flatness, small, though the arms are huge.
If I searched I would find *teenage* draped

over a heart & *boy* slunk over a shelf,
head resting on the shin of
a dear friend.

It's true I did go looking
in the cafeteria freezer, the stairs
to the parking lot, the yearbook. Next
to you in the photo, his face is cropped
close enough that your cheeks are
almost pressing.

The Stranger

Self-awareness is a wonderful thing.

Had a dream in which one
artery was wearing a ball cap, suffocating
blood flow, lidding.

—

A pair of punk gloves, no fingers.
One glove for you, one for him, half
and half, best-friend necklaces.

Your teacher wrote: *yours is a unique
approach and your writing works
in a gruesome way—*

*Good details & mood setting. C+ because
of run-ons.*

—

I hate you people for leaving me out of so many fun things. And
no don't fucking say, "well thats your fault" because it isn't, you
people had my phone #, and I asked and all, but no
no no no don't let the weird looking KID come along, ohh fucking
nooo.

Transcript: Basement Tape

In a video: a boy with long hair.
Strong nose, beaded hemp
necklace. A black coat slapping
the floor near ankles. Pulls
it onto his shoulders: "I'm fat

on this side." A glare ruins the shot

by his temple, elbow folds
into a *v* near the pocket like
a leather wishbone. "I'm fat

with all this stuff on," levels
a hand against his stomach.

Light dilates and he gets shot
through the lens straightforward.
"I'll have to take the coat off." Ball

cap backward, eyes slide behind
the frame; past it, beyond it, above
it, around it. Lips turn upside down
into a tight smile, he looks for a way

to make eye contact. There is no
other voice in response, though
the camera is shaking.

Before and After Peril

The wind makes the trees move on their insides.
On the floor in the library

the fragile bookshelf is pressing its spines into
the curve at the back of your heads. It

broke. There was no refraction of light & the stellar
became compacted. Once, I let myself
be thrown over a stranger's shoulder. He

carried me up concrete stairs and laid me
in a field where thorns supported my weight.
I reached back and felt your baseball caps,
soaked in blood, flattened by the detonation. I

reached and I failed. Someone pulls a white
sheet over & I'm unsure about the whiteness.
Whose cheek is on my leg. And which hand
is on my lungs. We are so small & red, red, collapsing.

Helix

That you may have been small, gene. A tiny cross
of parental freeways. Little fragment of extended
tastes: likes, dislikes, hair color, eyes.
That our thrills could be found in the departure—
a face wearing full honesty, and the winters
pressing our earrings out
of our ears. It is only winter we have
to sort our inadequacies against the snow,
amber dress, gold ring—as teenagers
we blew invisible candles on plastic cakes,
fingertip to fingertip on the kitchen counter.
Had we both been planned? Our happening.
Our ways. The proteins of our limbs.
Why not braids or beehives? We know
our chemical halves, our sum totals. Here we are:
each organic impulses of each; white cursive
on mirrors: are we here.

Muscle Memory

Trying to say your names midflight
back to Pittsburgh. Had to call you back
from a tight space, i.e. the cross of an *x,*
heat of a lung, quickness of a young breath
after running.

Forgot the sound of what is not exactly
you. A certain capacity of air vibrations
shaking down decibels. There are you two,

and then there is the story of you, and then
there are more bullets.

Why do anything with a dark reincarnate?
Answer: it's a sequence. Answer: it's the measure

of damage, the width of the wingspan,
the radiant shatter of airspace
as we fly straight toward a hook
in the most beautiful of blue skies.

But the Ghosts

Squinting through the aisle
turning a display with my index finger

a gloss named *Midsummer*
caught my eye

The remainders
of a barrel of lipstick

a pearl residue
shimmering in the depression

of the tube
I put it up to my eye

looked in

and together we
fell to the ground

like two flash floods
closing in on a parked car

I didn't know we
hadn't fainted

this wasn't daysleep

As it happened
I didn't know

men or illusions
of safety

and suddenly knew
the underside of infinity

in which one could
be crushed

into a display case
of eyeshadows

by a man
she didn't know

again and again
the damned migration

of my body:
from standing

to linoleum floor
A friction

I was.

Hold My Wrist

In 7th grade, I had a reoccurring dream about a man in a mime costume. I was sure I could hear him. God, the terror of the white face closing in toward mine. Who do we call for when the walls break open and somewhere a candle is lit in a séance? Through and through of it. Once I started a fire with a magnifying glass. It burst open like waves in the ocean. Who knows what makes our faces warm after shouting. It is the most tender I've ever felt. I can't speak for the mime or the acrobat, but by bending, I have fallen so completely down: a heavy rope dropped straight into the sea.

We drove looking for ghosts on the gravel road

high school boys: a stone inside means
I want to tell this story

a stone inside
a car I was

barely breaking into frost
& flowers of ice
chipped our bumpers

We put the windows down
to reach our wolf spirits

We follow another car
all over my body it is snowing

I lean to call out the window to you
choke on my blonde

hair I'll call you: *spirit*
I called you back from the shoulder

of a highway, plum
sunset tapering to a splinter

It is hard to know anything
wild-eyed

the brake light shadow
forms a blush on my cheek

Journal

I drew a shame then I drew a shame

Initials inside a heart on a notebook page

I drew your heart made a cross then wrote my name

They lose their bodies because there are no locks on the doors

I lost my body though it was great to think about you

and I and love

I drew a sign for fate then I drew fate

An asterisk or a cross with an *x* through it

A star or an *x* with a cross through it

I didn't know if I should call you or wait for fate to act

I didn't know if I should call you or wait for

A stem of the heart is a tapering road

I drew a road and I led it up into a heart

I drew hearts and in them stitches and in them hands

Emotional Intelligence

The fibers in the carpet
were so swollen
with blood, they tore
them up and replaced them.

The grass dried out for the third time
since March & in May it will still
be bright, bright, concealing.

*

Inside, she hoists herself

up   you bright dove

you leave

your eeyore & winnie

watch under a desk chair

push away melted calculators

make a run for it

*

Today, I am ten days into being twelve.
I avoid boys & shave my legs
using too much gel, let it dry
into a perfume. My legs
are slim & full of tropical.

Had to try, a girl has to try.
Lock the stall door in the bathroom,
wash the scent from our legs with damp toilet paper,
quick avoidance of a mirror.

That mirror glass. Bent back from kinetic discharge—
it cracked, it snapped, it spilled everywhere.

Witness

Couldn't help but read
you said *race* and see a vein

a vein & a library full of breath
hot against an earlobe

a boy crouching to see
who is underneath a table

O it is happening
come here to be with me

God dammit
here we are   here they are

we all are together
& how moonless

The gun is pointed
beneath the table

& you said *race*
& I heard *vein*

& no one made any
sound at all.

They were coming
the whole time,
but you didn't know:

the glass, the bone,
the way the chest—

I didn't even know
I was alive until

the last moment
in which your face
became a gold slit fraying

Red Earth

With more urgency
than I've grown to allow,

I am contesting
your eyes in a dream.
A panic of violas
rises behind us.
That stare, a sun of quiet.

In the vast slope of spring,
knowing how pale the wisteria gets

knowing your ankle as slender,
as less and less of it—

or do I know this? We
wait for each other in
the slopes of our backs. We
press the slopes of our backs.
We press into each other
& in the waiting: rage.

Who can blame our bodies
for taking. I take you & in
the taking the heat cracks
my knuckles.

Library Version

We shelve books with spines here, wood shelf. Boyfriends, girl-friends. A boy in cargo pants, a student, seventeen, a table. A gun and a bomb. All of us have book bags with notes with hearts at the bottom. April 1999. Prom kids. Two boys, boy, boy. Black boots, thin pants with big pockets. All of us have problems changing in front of each other for gym class. He was in love with. We've had mirrors in our lockers for a long time. He walked on the top of the table. A chair to conceal and a face. You see how under. You see us under. He was in love with. No chair, that is the secret, he flung it away. He said hey everybody. No trench coat, that is the secret, he bent down. He said hey everybody. His upside-down face, natural selection, long hair in the girls' bathroom. You look just like you but not alive. You see us under. He bent over. Hey. Carpet is cleaned under the tables. Kids with fibers, hey everybody, a wood shelf with spines.

Jefferson County

No one was unloved. Newspaper clippings split
up on the page like busted lips; they swell.
Written in the margin: *These are all white boys*

Just below is a photo of Andrew Golden & a headline:
Bloodlust video games put kids in the crosshairs.
You've been a sheep pushed against a metal shearer?
Bald, bracing the grass & surrounded
by fragments. Yes, bareness. Uncover.
Austere light of afternoon in Colorado. *All*

white. There are moments of bonding & then
there is direct contact. You have so little grace
& the sky it hurts

to look at. All the photographs are
tongues & teeth, animals wrestling
other animals. Last time I visited Colorado,
we walked by a police canine training facility.
Hundreds of dogs were barking & for miles
it was all you could hear, at least thirty dogs just crying
into the bombs & cancers & cocaine samples
they were learning to detect.

Kisses and kisses, the TSA woman
said to her friend when we flew out.
Show us how to leave you. Show us mesas throwing
orange dust onto highways, the Rockies as a terrace.
Show us the savage blue of yonder, and yonder as a means
of escaping the slip & fall, the tipping-over point,
the things we brace against when we consider
what is *just* or *unjust.*

Flood Water

I, too, stole something. Heard a swell
when you walked through water set off by a fire alarm,
circling the cafeteria, drinking from abandoned Pepsi cans.

*

So it is
to imagine
a shooting traveling
toward us, parting the dust
in the air, the pale fate
of a bullet   a pierce
       I'm wearing my hair
       in a ponytail

Parents say: here I come
here I come

here
is the word *threshold*
let us stand helplessly by

O the elegant doves
& the sheep with their white eyes open

Through the science lab window

Into this classroom we run
to the windows

& the girl who one day
used a three-ring binder
turns to see your strange eyes

she opens   she opens

turn the light off
see one face

turn it on
see two faces

she is suspended over
a lunch tray
it is overflowing with red flowers:

things that are beautiful, then die.
we can't look at your limping
or your little face

Here is a projection machine

something is coming

with four irises and a gun
they did it again
they did it again

This is a terrific moment
for her   reinvented

the precious
illuminate

her mouth   her painted nails

luminous girl
& twice the precise bullet

Landscape: Witness Report

If you kept going, you would have fallen over the textbook. You would have broken the cover.

She got so close she saw your acne. She couldn't help but stare at the blood on your teeth. Had a vision of someone hitting their own eyes, hands in fists, while the sprinklers rained down for hours and hours. Soft water-foam lapping.

You didn't wear contact lenses. The witness, the stranger, the tangible. Paperbacks are soaking wet. Goodbye, there is so much that goes on without you. There were intense moments of palsy after everything really began. Goodbye, there is so much.

Indoor Voices

In the middle of class she stops her lecture.
Out of the circle of desks, she sees him, a hive
falling into the mouths of other students. Broke
open.

Are we too weak to say the word *violent*

Are we trying not to embarrass anyone

He felt so brutal in his vulnerability

He builds and builds each day, more of a gap than she can handle,
splitting the classroom into speckled, dark contusions.
We keep going, rotate & reshape, bluer and bluer   a bruise

He presses, breaking vessels:
the most riveting bruise, dammit   rivet

She considers how language has such sincere consequences. How far
it can go   contract   expand

When his essays are turned in, they say *violent*
in asterisks all across the page. Goddamn, has the world
ever needed a woman to be so riveting?

Homeroom

It felt strange to return to this space
the next day, or rather this concept:

a room meant as a home
for small enlisted selves
marching to their gym
classes or math classes,
using Trapper Keepers

calling out to each other
after brushing their hair from
their Bonne Bell lip glosses—
for me it was root beer
also pink lemonade—

we sat two to a desk,
pledged allegiance toward
a tiny speaker hoisted
above our heads

Please know that we
thought about it

things were said
about zero tolerance,
codes & terms of conduct

Maybe there was a school-wide assembly
where I was precisely measuring
the distance of my body to Tim's,

or loosely braiding Martha's
hair. Please know we thought

about it in a way that rearranged
our schedules, in a way we
couldn't get out of, it was all

we could do, we lit the halls
up wondering who was suspicious

we listened to Mr. Austen
shut the classroom door first thing

that morning, we glanced
toward our windows to measure
the drop, we felt our bodies hum
touching shoulders during fire drills,
we mentioned metal detectors, we
noticed boys' hair, we noticed the color
black, we noticed each other's
hands, we noticed each other

Day Zero

after Simon Armitage

Somewhere in a cafeteria, I will enter
with stars pointed directly at the girls at the back
table, mark them with five-points to the tips of their
hairs, spectrum grazing from ear to
cheek. When you round the corner from the hallway,
give me your extra stars, there is someone
who cannot refuse one, stinging tattoo constellation.
Then we can leave for the gym. We won't hold hands,
but our stars will be interlocked with plasma and dust,
the basketball hoop a tiny dipper of solar burns.
Coach with a star behind his knee, did you do that?
The balls are in a deflated galaxy under
the bleachers—I just saw someone run to the metal exits.
Now they are bright with gravity: we gave
them a star for the back of their T-shirt.
Let's go together to the library and we still
won't hold hands, I will paint a sun on your temple—
no, no you will draw a comet on your
forehead while I lean against the orbiting shelves.

Cliff Theory

Every bone is burning a cool fire,
joints like magnetic asterisks grinding
deeper, our dense axis. We are so heavy.

It is over, we two are sitting, backs pressed
to low shelves of books. I'm right behind
your long & bright arms.

*

I see your temple as a sequence
of elements becoming an
expanding planet, pulsing
with a core and mass. It has its own
system: rings, moonlets, gravity,
but no stars. I give you a star

for this planet. There is dust and ice in
the back of my throat. I drew a fate
then I drew a fate in my mouth.

I wanted to live, of course—

but later, sitting on top of a bed

I heard myself tell a friend
that it was more about seeing
the mirrors in the cosmetics aisle
upside down

how curious it was to be flipped

to see the world with this new, toppling
authority: lip glosses pouring forth
as my legs kicked a display case

She nodded with concern: *did anyone
see what happened?*

I talked about mirrors again:

well,
the reflections knew.

Iterations of the event playing out
in vast multitudes of tiny drugstore
mirrors: quantum universes
showing me, upside down, his
face, then my face,
my hair pulled tight in a ponytail—
you smell so nice
in strange reverb.

My extravagance, I told my friend.

It was, after all, because I wanted a new blush.

She laughed: *god, that is so weird.*
We downloaded a song from Limewire.

Security cameras, those too, I wanted
to say. They also saw what happened.

Afterward, spinning from the acceleration
of my heartbeat, I burst

from the aisle, searching
for real eyes to acknowledge

what they had seen in the mirrors, what
happened to me in them.

Did you see that version?

The same version I saw?
Of me, but not me—
the warped eyeshadows

falling around us into tiny
piles of glitter ash, my hands
still sparkling the next day

at some point. glosses
rolling under his feet

Did you see that version?
Or hear it from the next
aisle? *You look so nice today*
with a small crash

My gravity upended
but caught in a suspension
of glass echoes:

could the store have been floating
or was I being dragged

I left my friend's house later
wondering if it was funny

After all: we'd laughed

though I could feel the humming
of fluorescence behind my eyes,
still light-stung

the powder of a blush
staining my T-shirt rose.

Sleepwalking after CCD

It smelled like soap when
you were talking about the
trinity

I came through the
swallow of tall grass,
equal parts blank, red,
sanded:

I was equal parts
& emerging from the
neighbor's guest
house—I saw you
standing

in the pitch black like
a   nightingale,
nightingale   you've
ruined

my sleep but
it smelled as close
to a shower

You'll make up
for your own
death

every night
standing &
floating
with jesus & the spirit

there is no choice
it gets colder around 6

here is our little
scene near the
unmade
lawn you
scared me when
I was just at that age

Periphery

My favorite artery
I understood was
dusk to the rest
of the body.

Set back, growing dim,
it pulsed: a gray hour
of oxygen—could it be

mid-winter within
him? Shaking
out a muscle: we

are somewhere
averting. We are
backwards or in
a trance or in a
dioxide stargazing.

From the self:
duress

metallic echo—
your whole self
sending back its
savage necessities.

Imagining an Aftermath

Some time passes, you go back to your paper
kingdom and close your eyes.
Maybe you've been lucky
in the dark, no one sees your fingers growing teeth.
We will not understand the coring
of your body—all that love! There it goes! The tonsils were not
worth it. The mountains were not worth it. The eyelashes,
the shoulders. You filled the earth ten
times over with a slanted eye. Pain, meet the pain
of one string, of one straight line from hand to brain to gun.

There's more. Just left behind from sleep. A *please*.

A *desire*. A hand cupping a bad heart. A hole in a paper skull
called into again: salt, or pale, or imploding.

Springtime

Maybe we are leaving
together, not hiding

Let's speak through
the wall, the bare floor. Come
over to be with me

I've been listening so many
years how
to know   how to know

to fail at touching

your cheek
as the day splits
at the window, settles
in   why do you trust
me

& your eyes—beating

Perennial

Feels like daytime on my muscles; early teen, quite thin.

I went to see *The Secret Garden,* waited for the campfire scene,
pulled smoke near until I breathed it. I really breathed it, & you.
Our place in the theater is overgrown & petals are falling off
down the aisles: it looks like a gun just happened in the movie.
Your gun a ghost silhouetted on a screen & played out in slow
motion. This should be menacing.

I hit the floor heavy with thorns; crawl on my palms collecting
tiny spikes—so small my palms, tendons sharp and cut up.

Right behind, you're grabbing my leg & pressing your cheek to
my calf & kissing. I'll always

let this happen. I hope always—my hands are brittle flowers,
breaking all over.

The Journal of the Girls

I need to take the top off one more time.
("What top?") The top of me.

—Ryann Wahl

She took the skin off the rock. Sat up
from sunbathing to watch a man running sideways

her hair soft lighter fluid
I know there is no love there
in the careful observation

a violet fog rolling up past her calves
she bites her wrist vein, quicksilver, brings
it to the mouth of the grass

void me, void me
the steepness of breath inside
I know this glass body
diamond bone
it is mine; also, yours; ours,
I recognize it all

You caught the bright in your center
You clot the finite in your

painted nails. So temporary. Silk
eyelashes, will you watch for me

—

In a sheet tent, here is the flashlight

divine hair of your sister cut
into kidney shapes

Two hearts in hot ringlets

Here in this humid orchestra
she plays with her fingers:
shadow-puppet rabbits
in between webbing the smell
of apple cores

you both should be rising

and twinkling against the cotton
should be braiding the pulp
of your leftover tea

why is no one moving

is this the silhouette of a burial
or are we still swimming
in the lake beside Pennsylvania

Slow Burn

At first there were too many gold moons,
so he clips them. Then it was spring.
In the poppies, a tiny black umbrella opens.
Beneath it, the boy with scissors, moving forward.

We watch as the umbrella moves out of the poppies
and onto linoleum. There is no careful way to say:
he wants to be a sun and the sun
wants to do something helpful. We can hear

his shoes, and suddenly—another.
A woman with a hood. *Do you know it is raining?*
The umbrella stops, drops. *No, everything.* Here:
a hand reaching to touch a cheek. What is this

exchange? He, the sun; you, the skin; she, the bird.
No, everything. If he could build a bullet, she could
wrap the bullet in his shirt. His chest. Slate pearl in a soft
cushion. We've been watching for a long time: the sky

is gray as a throat. Our lungs slap our bones,
the linoleum frosts over.
Here is the tunnel dim-lit inside of me.
You were. You were so hysterical.

Part Nocturne

I say good-night
to all the things
in my bedroom:
good-night blinds, good-night
closet, crème walls.

Window air cooled
my legs burning
with eczema, the dark
rusting around my girl
body like a metal shell
seared, hair soldered
into wires on a pillow.

I asked the night to weld
lesions on my shins
to its tender casing,
melt a veil to heal
my injured skin,

in the dim I asked
to be released from sore
and raw to sleep off
the tarnish circled by black

I am sere, firmed
with wear-and-tear
resistance. Under my nails
I hold the blanket and wish it
good-night

intimate berceuse
sealing me over.

Portrait

Someone claims you wrote *I hate you*
in Wite-Out across your bag's front
pocket a week before. There is no way

to explain the silence of that. How
suspicious the air feels when it's just
been cut open. Your acceptance
into the University of Arizona. A
job at Blackjack Pizza, picture
from prom, Rammstein. An asterisk
piercing a window, letting the sun in.

No matter the entanglements, your halves
hovering like needles over an arm—
no matter the witness & how collected
or uncollected: you grew up in front
of a whole school. The ever-suiciding
starlings we pick up to cradle and drop
again and again with lessening mercy.

March

I've never been part of a procession.
The arrow of my bone to her bone
didn't lead us in a straight line.
We didn't walk forward or into
anything.

If there was ice, I avoided it. There
was iron in a birch tree—it was straining
our earlobes. It was turning our blood dark.

She couldn't have been smaller.
If she felt fear, it was a pale blue circle
treading around a center of gray. In this
recollection, there is a lapse in the lime

dust of gravel and melting snow.
Its settlement. It is a long arcing story
of losing and moving into white noise
with that loss. Moving backward. With terrific rigidity.

Reunion

we were born in sunlight
a birth in clovers
behind our birdbath

I dreamt my sister
near a chain-link fence
inherited a horse

and that I conjured a snake from its mane

no poison, just a slim, bitter fang
attached to scales attached to muscles

we each took an ax
and swung, splitting it into halves
—suddenly it was glass, as flowers
bursting open in spring, everywhere

uncontrollable glass. The cinders
froze in terror. The horse looked
away. I am not fearing

this power. Wood blisters, bring us home.
Venom splinters, bring us, golden field
bring us, flaring sun bring us,
mercury blade bring the cleanest cut
to the leanest lung and home.

Notes

Some language in "1999" and "The Stranger" is adapted from the Columbine report, Jefferson County Sheriff's Department.

"Transcript: Basement Tape" references a video recording of Dylan Klebold and Eric Harris dated March 15, 1999.

"Cliff Theory" is described in Dylan Klebold's personal journal with the remarks: "The cliff theory . . . everyone trying to get higher & stable" and "many people climbing up a never-ending vertical cliff . . . [edited] & [edited] found a plateau to exist on . . . they walked up me to get to it. Nobody will help me." There is also an accompanying sketch to further illustrate Klebold's descriptions.

Acknowledgments

Thank you to the following publications in which these poems have appeared (in some version):

American Poets: "A poem in which I am dreaming" and "Cliff Theory"

Black Warrior Review: "Historical Documents"

Columbia Poetry Review: "Perennial" and "1999"

DIAGRAM: "A poem in which I am dreaming"

Floating Wolf Quarterly: "We drove looking for ghosts on the gravel road"

iO: "No, Everything"

The Pinch: "Hold My Wrist" and "Colorado, Hunting"

Pinwheel: "Imagining an Aftermath"

Pittsburgh Tribune (North Hills reprint): "A poem in which I am dreaming"

So much gratitude to the writing community at Columbia College Chicago—particularly Tony Trigilio and David Trinidad. Jaswinder Bolina, you have remained a touchstone of my poetic process since day one; thank you for your honesty, support, and guidance. Many thanks to Antonio Caruso for over a decade of encouragement.

Deep thanks to Caroline, Mandy, Nica, Chris, Erika, Carla, and the whole team at Coffee House Press for bringing this book into the world with such great care. Lizzie Davis, I am indebted to your incredible editorial eye.

Thank you to Holly Amos, Hafizah Geter, and Ryann Stevenson for stargazing with me and showing me all the potentialities of poetry (and friendship). Lizzie Harris, from sitting cross-legged in the hallways of the Cathedral of Learning at Pitt waiting for our first poetry workshop to begin, to now—you are one of the best editors I know.

Thank you Martha Fitzgerald, lifelong partner in crime, coauthor of "Generation Next." Kristie McVay, from my first open mic night at the Shadow Lounge, you have been there—thank you for encouraging me at every turn. Erin Holmes, you've never missed any of my readings, or an opportunity to root for this book: thank you.

Thank you to Jan Beatty, Chrissy Price, Molly Holmes, Megan Kochin, Janessa Jackson, Emily Bengel, Rachel Strittmatter, Meghan McQuiggan, Joanna Klink, Camille Rankine, Brenda Shaughnessy, Craig Morgan Teicher, Alex Dimitrov, Deborah Landau, James Arthur, Lynn Emanuel, Matthew Zapruder, Dawn Lundy Martin, Ocean Vuong, Lisa Olstein, Jericho Brown, Dana Jennings, Alex Crowley, Jay Deshpande, Ben Purkert, Will Brewer, Lindsay Bernal, Kima Jones, Melissa Faliveno, Dana Levin, Mark Bibbins, Stephen Danos, Jeff Oaks, Jessica Campbell, Tomás Q. Morín, Dean Rader, Cat Richardson, Brian Russell, Ricardo Maldonado, Ellen Bass, Ellen Silverstein, Jordan Valdés, Simon Marteli, Colette and Joe Sharbaugh, Elaina Ellis, Emily Grise, Janeen Armstrong, Joseph Bednarik, Michael Wiegers, George Knotek, Tonaya Craft, Victoria Poling, and the University of Maryland Jiménez-Porter Writers' House team.

So many thanks to my beloved National Geographic crew, the Rathbuns, the Andersens, the Harris family, the Miller family, the Fitzgeralds, the Hopeys, the Silversteins, the Annibales, my dear Sarah Miller, Gina, David, Bella, and Dr. Fayaz Shawl.

My parents, Romaine and Jack, and my sister, Morgan: "I hope you know" how much I love you, and how much of this book is a result of your support.

Jonathan Shawl, my partner on this planet, and in all the universes seen and unseen: thank you.

Coffee House Press began as a small letterpress operation in 1972 and has grown into an internationally renowned nonprofit publisher of literary fiction, essay, poetry, and other work that doesn't fit neatly into genre categories.

Coffee House is both a publisher and an arts organization. Through our *Books in Action* program and publications, we've become interdisciplinary collaborators and incubators for new work and audience experiences. Our vision for the future is one where a publisher is a catalyst and connector.

LITERATURE
is not the same thing as
PUBLISHING

Funder Acknowledgments

Coffee House Press is an internationally renowned independent book publisher and arts nonprofit based in Minneapolis, MN; through its literary publications and *Books in Action* program, Coffee House acts as a catalyst and connector—between authors and readers, ideas and resources, creativity and community, inspiration and action.

Coffee House Press books are made possible through the generous support of grants and donations from corporations, state and federal grant programs, family foundations, and the many individuals who believe in the transformational power of literature. This activity is made possible by the voters of Minnesota through a Minnesota State Arts Board Operating Support grant, thanks to the legislative appropriation from the arts and cultural heritage fund. Coffee House also receives major operating support from the Amazon Literary Partnership, the Jerome Foundation, McKnight Foundation, Target Foundation, and the National Endowment for the Arts (NEA). To find out more about how NEA grants impact individuals and communities, visit www.arts.gov.

Coffee House Press receives additional support from the Elmer L. & Eleanor J. Andersen Foundation; the David & Mary Anderson Family Foundation; Bookmobile; the Buuck Family Foundation; Fredrikson & Byron, P.A.; Dorsey & Whitney LLP; the Fringe Foundation; Kenneth Koch Literary Estate; the Knight Foundation; the Matching Grant Program Fund of the Minneapolis Foundation; Mr. Pancks' Fund in memory of Graham Kimpton; the Schwab Charitable Fund; Schwegman, Lundberg & Woessner, P.A.; the U.S. Bank Foundation; and VSA Minnesota for the Metropolitan Regional Arts Council.

The Publisher's Circle of Coffee House Press

Publisher's Circle members make significant contributions to Coffee House Press's annual giving campaign. Understanding that a strong financial base is necessary for the press to meet the challenges and opportunities that arise each year, this group plays a crucial part in the success of Coffee House's mission.

Recent Publisher's Circle members include many anonymous donors, Suzanne Allen, Patricia A. Beithon, the E. Thomas Binger & Rebecca Rand Fund of the Minneapolis Foundation, Andrew Brantingham, Robert & Gail Buuck, Claire Casey, Louise Copeland, Jane Dalrymple-Hollo, Mary Ebert & Paul Stembler, Kaywin Feldman & Jim Lutz, Chris Fischbach & Katie Dublinski, Sally French, Jocelyn Hale & Glenn Miller, the Rehael Fund-Roger Hale/Nor Hall of the Minneapolis Foundation, Randy Hartten & Ron Lotz, Dylan Hicks & Nina Hale, William Hardacker, Randall Heath, Jeffrey Hom, Carl & Heidi Horsch, Amy L. Hubbard & Geoffrey J. Kehoe Fund, Kenneth Kahn & Susan Dicker, Stephen & Isabel Keating, Kenneth Koch Literary Estate, Cinda Kornblum, Jennifer Kwon Dobbs & Stefan Liess, Lambert Family Foundation, Lenfestey Family Foundation, Sarah Lutman & Rob Rudolph, the Carol & Aaron Mack Charitable Fund of the Minneapolis Foundation, George & Olga Mack, Joshua Mack & Ron Warren, Gillian McCain, Malcolm S. McDermid & Katie Windle, Mary & Malcolm McDermid, Sjur Midness & Briar Andresen, Maureen Millea Smith & Daniel Smith, Peter Nelson & Jennifer Swenson, Enrique & Jennifer Olivarez, Alan Polsky, Marc Porter & James Hennessy, Robin Preble, Alexis Scott, Ruth Stricker Dayton, Jeffrey Sugerman & Sarah Schultz, Nan G. & Stephen C. Swid, Kenneth Thorp in memory of Allan Kornblum & Rochelle Ratner, Patricia Tilton, Joanne Von Blon, Stu Wilson & Melissa Barker, Warren D. Woessner & Iris C. Freeman, Margaret Wurtele, and Wayne P. Zink & Christopher Schout.

For more information about the Publisher's Circle and other ways to support Coffee House Press books, authors, and activities, please visit www.coffeehousepress.org/support or contact us at info@coffeehousepress.org.

KELLY FORSYTHE's poetry has been published in the *American Poetry Review*, the *Literary Review*, the *Minnesota Review*, and *Columbia Poetry Review*, among others. She was recently featured in *American Poets* as an Academy of American Poets Emerging Poet, with an introduction by Noelle Kocot. Forsythe was the director of publicity for Copper Canyon Press for over half a decade. She has taught workshops for the Jiménez-Porter Writers' House at the University of Maryland and American University and works for National Geographic in Washington, DC.

Perennial was designed by
Bookmobile Design & Digital Publisher Services.
Text is set in Dante MT Pro.